LEADS TO NOWHERE

Leads to Nowhere

Healing Through Encounters with the Quantum

BRIANNA LAFFERTY

Bri0nic LLC

Contents

Why I needed to write this third book...

When I typed up my near-death experience in the pages of my first award-winning book, "White Flame," I sensed there was another chapter waiting to be told. And true enough, just a few months later, I found myself collaborating with my mom on my second book, "Wired to be Dysfunctional," chronicling our tumultuous journey with Myoclonus Dystonia.

Initially, I saw these two stories as separate pieces in the puzzle of my life, each significant in its own right. However, as I delved deeper into the intricacies of my experiences, I began to unravel the hidden connections that bound them together in a divine dance of synchronicity.

The realization struck me like a bolt of lightning: these seemingly disparate narratives were not only linked, but intricately intertwined, weaving together to form a larger picture of interconnectedness and purpose.

And so, driven by the profound insight of this revelation, I felt compelled to share my story with the world. Thus, "Leads to Nowhere" was born—a testament to the power of interconnectedness, resilience, healing, and the transformative journey of self-discovery.

Dive into the depths of intertwined stories, exploring the magic of life's interconnectedness and the profound wisdom it holds. Embark on a journey of healing, understanding, and the boundless possibilities that arise when we enter Nowhere.

Chapter 1

Too Much for a
Ten Year Old

The start of this tale doesn't unfold with the typical, "I was just a regular ten-year-old" narrative. No, it's more like a sudden onslaught of sheer terror that crashed into my world all at once, leaving me breathless and bewildered. It wasn't just a passing storm; it felt like it would engulf me forever.

Reflecting on it now, I realize that every twist and turn, every moment of terror and turmoil, had its purpose and its place in the grand scheme of things. It's as if fate orchestrated each event with precision, leading me down a path of growth and understanding.

At the tender age of ten, my family made the decision to relocate to Colorado, settling in a seemingly innocuous little town on the Eastern plains. This move would mark the beginning of a harrowing chapter in my life. Leaving behind the bustling city life where my sister and I were surrounded by friends, we entered a world where making a single friend felt like an insurmountable challenge.

But it wasn't just the loneliness that weighed heavily on my young shoulders. I soon found myself a target of relentless bullying at my new school, ostracized in a close-knit community where I felt like an outsider. While my external struggles mirrored those of many others, it was the turmoil brewing within me that threatened to consume my very essence.

Around this time, I began having odd and unfamiliar symptoms. As strange sensations began creeping into my prepubescent life, my parents brushed them off as part of growing up. But to me, it felt like my body was betraying me in ways I couldn't understand. My forearms and calves would throb and cramp relentlessly, day and night, leaving me writhing in pain. I'd try to hide my discomfort by wrapping them tightly with ACE bandages, hoping to conceal the agony and embarrassment beneath my clothes. Nightly, I found myself trapped in a torment of charlie horses, despite my wholesome kid's diet. The pain was relentless, unyielding, and seemed to grow more intense with each passing day.

But it wasn't just physical pain that plagued me; nightmares and insomnia clawed their way into my nights. I'd toss and turn until the wee hours of the morning, my mind swirling with fear and exhaustion. I kept my struggles a secret from my parents, convinced they wouldn't understand the darkness that consumed my nights.

When sleep finally came, it brought with it a twisted realm of terror. I was haunted by relentless nightmares of being chased, attacked, and ensnared in a web of fear. The horrors intensified like clockwork, every July and December, a pattern that would take years to unravel.

And as if the weight of these burdens wasn't enough for a girl on the cusp of puberty, my new home harbored secrets of its own. Paranormal occurrences danced on the edges of my reality, a surreal and unsettling addition to my already turbulent world.

I encountered harmless ghosts at first, their spectral forms passing through my vision with eerie nonchalance. But soon, the benign turned malevolent, as I found myself face-to-face with dark entities that sent shivers down my spine.

One chilling encounter remains etched in my memory: the night I ventured into the guest bedroom, only to find an old doll, its eyeless gaze and lifeless body turning, and following my every move with glowing red intensity.

From that moment on, the room held a sinister allure I dared not revisit.

In the darkness of our basement, a shadowy figure with a top hat and cape prowled the walls, a silent sentinel of dread. It would take two decades to uncover the truth and the significance behind this haunting apparition.

These encounters, though terrifying, would shape my perception of reality in ways I couldn't comprehend at the time. Despite societal skepticism and familial disbelief, I knew in my heart that the paranormal was real, and its mysteries held untold power.

In the eyes of my ten-year-old self, I embraced the notion that magic was real, that unseen energies and mysteries lurked beyond the veil of the mundane world. Little did I know, this belief would set the stage for an extraordinary journey of self-discovery and empowerment that lay ahead.

Chapter 2

In the Shadows of Despair

As adolescence dawned, the world around me seemed to dim, swallowed by a darkness that mirrored the turmoil within. The shadows deepened with each passing day, casting a heavy rain cloud over my existence that I couldn't shake.

The strange symptoms that plagued me grew in both number and intensity, a relentless assault on my fragile body. Nerve pain tore through me like bolts of lightning, leaving me squirming in agony. My muscles clenched with such ferocity that walking became a Herculean task, my back rigid as a fortress wall. I jerked violently, as if I was being administered unexpected volts into my extremities. These were later classified as non epileptic myoclonic seizures.

The tremors that wracked my body were like an arctic chill, leaving me shivering and trembling as if I'd been plunged into the icy depths of the North Pole, clad only in a flimsy swimsuit. But it wasn't just the physical torment that weighed on me; the psychological toll was equally crushing.

Anxiety gripped me in its vice-like embrace, its relentless grip tightening around my chest until it felt like my heart was racing a million miles a minute, ready to burst free from its confines. Depression weighed on me like a suffocating wet blanket, dragging me down into a swamp of despair. Obsessive-Compulsive Disorder (OCD) thoughts spiraled endlessly in my mind, a relentless cycle of obsessions that threatened to consume me whole.

Seeking solace, my mom and I turned to medical professionals, hoping for answers that never seemed to come. Instead of clarity, we were met with confusion and misdiagnosis; trapped in a maze of dangerous pharmaceutical cocktails that only exacerbated my suffering. With each doctor's visit came a sinking realization: no one had the answers I so desperately sought.

The fear gnawed at me, a constant companion in the darkness that enveloped me. The thought of facing an uncertain future, plagued by unrelenting pain and anguish, filled me with a bone-deep terror. In those moments, all I wanted was to escape, to retreat into the comforting embrace of sleep and leave the nightmare of my reality behind.

But fate wasn't finished dealing its cruel blows, as if determined to add insult to injury. I became a prisoner of chronic and extreme insomnia, robbed of the solace of sleep that others took for granted. Night after night, I lay awake in the suffocating embrace of night, the minutes ticking by like agonizing eternities. The few hours of restless slumber I managed to steal in an attempt to escape my daily nightmares, were plagued by another onslaught of sleep-induced, horrific, nightmares that clawed at the fragile remnants of my sanity.

I reached out to therapists and counselors in a desperate bid for answers, but their reassurances fell flat in the face of my torment. They only added to the overwhelming negative experiences in my life. The nightmares, filled with terror and violence, tore through my psyche like a relentless storm, leaving me reeling in confusion and despair. How could I conjure such horrors when my waking life held no trace of such physical abuse?

The weight of my inexplicable nightmares bore down on me like a leaden blanket, suffocating my attempts to break free from my depression and anxiety. Each night brought a new onslaught of terror, leaving me wondering how I could ever find peace in a world so consumed by darkness.

And then, just when I thought I couldn't bear the burden of my nightmares any longer, I was confronted with a family secret that shattered the fragile illusion of my reality. An instance that involved me, buried deep within the recesses of my subconscious, waiting to be unearthed and laid bare for all to see. I was violated at a very young age which is why I could not consciously remember the event. Psychologists at the time had told my family that the event could show up again in puberty, either in my consciousness, or my subconsciousness. The subconscious often awakens in our dreams so it finally made sense. I also now understood why these dreams would worsen two times a year. I unknowingly started seeing the person who assaulted me again at the bi-yearly family reunions. Suddenly, it all made sense— the reason behind the escalating intensity of my nightmares, the insidious presence that haunted my dreams twice a year.

Unbeknownst to my conscious mind, my subconscious held the key to a dark secret buried deep within my past. Twice a year, like clockwork, I found myself face-to-face with my abuser, a chilling awakening of the trauma I had long suppressed. While I may not have recognized him consciously, my subconscious recognized the threat, sounding the alarm in the only way it knew how. Looking back, I realize that my dreams were a desperate plea for help, a silent scream echoing through the depths of my mind.

The weight of this revelation added another layer of complexity to an already tumultuous childhood, leaving me adrift in a sea of confusion and despair. Lost in a maze of hidden truths and buried memories, I continued to struggle to make sense of the relentless storm that enveloped me.

Chapter 3

Divine Decisions

There I stood, lost in a world of pain, fear, and isolation. Unbeknownst to me, I stood at a pivotal crossroads in my life, a moment pregnant with a decision that would shape my destiny in ways I couldn't yet fathom.

I observed those around me, their discomfort and pain often manifesting in harsh words and unkind actions. I felt the sting of their bitterness, the weight of their frustrations bearing down on others and myself. And in that moment, I made a choice—a choice that would set me apart from the darkness that threatened to consume me.

I resolved, with a determination born of necessity, that no matter the depth of my suffering, I would not allow it to dictate how I treated others. This decision, though seemingly insignificant at the time, would prove to be a beacon of light in the darkest of storms. For over 22 years, amidst the throes of pain and exhaustion, I held fast to this resolve, refusing to succumb to the temptation of bitterness and resentment.

A pivotal decision awaited me, a decision that would alter the trajectory of my journey in ways I could scarcely imagine. I refused to embrace the role of victimhood, despite the countless opportunities that presented themselves. People offered their sympathy, their pity, but I refused to accept it. Instead, I chose to uplift and empower those around me, reminding them of the significance of their own struggles.

I had plenty of opportunities to fall into the victim mindset with comments like, "I have this pain, but I'm sure it's not even comparable to yours," or "What you're going through is so much worse than me." Instead of taking these chances to take pity on myself, I took these chances to encourage and validate their journey too. I often replied, "If a paper cut was the worst pain you've ever experienced, and you have a paper cut right now, it's the most painful thing in your life right now. It's a 10 out of 10 for you. My pain is the worst I've ever experienced, so it is still a 10 out of 10 for me.

In this reply, I rejected the notion of comparison, recognizing that each journey is unique and valid in its own right. I refused to engage in the futile game of measuring pain, knowing all too well the limitations of the pain scale and its inability to capture the true essence of suffering.

In the face of adversity, I remained steadfast in my refusal to be labeled a victim. I refused to conform to society's expectations, to be reduced to a mere statistic on a pain scale. My journey was my own, and I refused to let anyone else define it for me.

The other decision I made during my teenage years was a crucial moment in my journey of survival. It stemmed from a deep-seated instinct to refuse to let things happen to me, a subconscious urge to adapt and overcome the challenges that threatened to consume me.

I found solace in art, losing myself in the delicate strokes of pencil sketches that brought emotions to life on paper. But as my condition worsened, and the constant tremors rendered my hands unsteady, I faced a devastating realization—I could no longer create the intricate artworks that once brought me joy.

Instead of succumbing to despair, I embraced adaptation as my lifeline. Photography became my new outlet, offering a medium where I could capture moments of beauty and emotion without the constraints of trembling hands. I poured myself into the art of capturing images, finding a new passion in the click of the shutter and the magic of developing film.

When the world of film began to fade into obsolescence, I shifted gears once again, finding solace in the vibrant hues of painting. Though my new creations lacked the finesse of my previous works, they provided a much-needed outlet for my emotions.

But adaptation wasn't limited to the realm of art. When muscle rigidity threatened to rob me of my mobility, I embraced the use of a cane, a tool I thought to be the least obvious. Though it was a source of embarrassment in the halls of high school, it was a necessary instrument in my fight for independence.

Despite the heartbreak and hardship that accompanied constant adaptation, each new challenge served as a stepping stone to resilience. It was through exploring new avenues and embracing change that I found the strength to endure another decade and a half of uncertainty.

In the years leading up to my diagnosis, I embarked on a journey of healing that spanned a myriad of modalities. From conventional pharmaceuticals to holistic treatments, I left no stone unturned in my quest for relief. While many approaches offered little respite from my symptoms, others left a lasting impact on my life.

One such influence came from my sessions with a hypnotist, who introduced me to the basics of Neuro-Linguistic Programming (NLP). Through his guidance, I learned the power of language and the importance of framing my thoughts and experiences in a positive light. This practice would prove invaluable in my healing journey, offering a pathway to lasting change and inner peace.

In addition to NLP, I also delved into the world of Eye Movement Desensitization and Reprocessing (EMDR) under the guidance of the hypnotist's wife. Through this transformative therapy, I discovered the keys to unlocking the chains of trauma that had bound me for so long. Armed with these newfound techniques, I embarked on a journey of healing and self-discovery, guided by the belief that freedom from pain and suffering was within my grasp.

Chapter 4

Embracing Shadows

Despite the relentless darkness that surrounded me, I defied the odds and not only graduated from high school but did so at the age of 16, all while grappling with the weight of my condition. School was a battleground I navigated with grit and determination, refusing to let my struggles define my future. Instead of succumbing to the allure of dropping out, I doubled down on my efforts, pushing myself to the limits to earn my diploma ahead of schedule.

With my sights set on a brighter tomorrow, I dove headfirst into a program at the local community college, eager to pursue my associate's degree. But the cloud of my mysterious symptoms loomed large, casting a shadow over my aspirations. With a less than optimistic prognosis, I took a step back from school after securing my Associates Degree. Despite the relentless insomnia that haunted my nights, I forged ahead, securing a job as a cashier at a grocery store to support myself.

My days blurred into nights as I toiled away, my insomnia a constant companion that refused to relent. Yet, in the depths of the night, I found comfort in an empty gym, the rhythmic clang of weights echoing my determination to persevere. As the world slept, I poured my heart and soul into each workout, a testament to my unwavering resolve.

But even amidst the chaos of my daily life, there was a glimmer of hope on the horizon—a ray of light in the form of a diagnosis. After 8 long years of uncertainty, a neurologist at Anschutz offered a beacon of clarity, identifying my condition as Myoclonus Dystonia. Finally, there was a name for the relentless storm raging within me, a label that encompassed the full spectrum of my physical and mental anguish. In the 8 years of searching for an answer, my mom thought it had to fit within the Occam's razor theory. In philosophy, Occam's razor is the problem-solving principle that recommends searching for explanations constructed with the smallest possible set of elements. The symptoms of anxiety, depression, OCD, insomnia, involuntary muscle movements, muscle rigidity, tremors, and pain were not the results of 8 different disorders, but one rare one. Instead of having a myriad of different disorders like the doctors had previously thought, all of my symptoms fit into one disorder, Myoclonus Dystonia.

I thought with a diagnosis, I would also get a solution. However, that was far from reality. Myoclonus Dystonia is a genetic neurological movement disorder that is incurable and very difficult to treat. By the time of diagnosis, I had already tried so many of the medications they use to treat Myoclonus Dystonia, with little to no relief. As it was a pretty new diagnosis and a very rare condition, little research was being done into this disorder. I had also tried a number of holistic and spiritual approaches to no avail. I tried a few more medications before my doctor's didn't know what else I could try and suggested I self-medicate with alcohol due to the fact the condition was also known as alcohol-responsive Myoclonus Dystonia.

As swift as the diagnosis came, the crushing realization that there was no cure, no easy fix to alleviate my suffering rushed in just as fast. Myoclonus Dystonia—a rare and incurable disorder—cast a shadow over my hopes for a better tomorrow. The tiny raft I had built myself on the foundation of hope for a normal future ended up leaving me adrift in a sea of uncertainty.

The whole journey with Myoclonus Dystonia is enough to fill a book in itself. Which is why I wrote a book about it! My mom and I co-authored "Wired to be Dysfunctional: Our Journey with Myoclonus Dystonia." It goes into depth about the first 21 years of having this disorder. We wrote the book thinking my condition finally had an answer and a resolution. We were premature.

Armed with nothing but sheer determination and an unyielding will to survive stemming from nothing more than being born hard-headed and stubborn as all get out, I continued on a journey of self-discovery, navigating the turbulent waters of life with courage. Though the shadows may have loomed large, I refused to let them consume me, finding love in the simple joys of everyday life. From the tranquility of a bubble bath to the comfort of a delightful beverage, these seemingly ordinary moments enveloped me like a warm blanket, offering relief amidst the turmoil.

For despite the darkness that threatened to engulf me, I remained steadfast in my resolve to emerge triumphant, to succeed at life, despite a progressively debilitating illness, a testament to the resilient power of the human spirit and pulling from strength one otherwise may never know they had.

Chapter 5

Adopting Change

After years of pouring my heart and soul into fixing up my home, navigating through unhealthy relationships, battling the relentless progression of my symptoms, and going back to school for my Bachelor's Degree, I knew it was time for a change. So, with a mixture of trepidation and excitement, I made the exciting decision to sell my house and embark on a new chapter of my life, alone, in San Antonio, TX.

Leaving behind the familiar comforts of Colorado, I set my sights on the unknown, driven by a deep-seated desire for change. With each passing mile, I felt a sense of liberation wash over me, a newfound freedom tinged with the promise of endless possibilities.

Arriving in San Antonio, I found myself mesmerized by the breathtaking beauty that surrounded me—a stunning apartment overlooking rolling hills and lush greenery. It was a sanctuary, a refuge from the chaos of my past, and I reveled in the serenity it hinted at.

Despite the challenges of isolation, pain, and chemical dependency that lay in front of me, I was determined to embrace this new chapter with open arms, seizing every opportunity to explore the vibrant city and immerse myself in its rich culture. From leisurely walks with my beloved dog to exhilarating motorcycle rides through the winding streets, each moment was an exciting change from my past.

Yet, amidst the excitement and adventure, I grappled with the daunting task of managing my symptoms with the dangerous, self-medicating advice that my doctors had recommended, and the often too common result of over-medicating. I attempted various programs, but they only intensified the overwhelming sense of powerlessness in my life. By then, Myoclonus Dystonia had already stripped away so much from me. The thought of a program attempting to diminish what little remained felt like a cruel blow, adding to the weight of despair already pressing down on me. It was a delicate dance, a constant struggle to find equilibrium in the midst of uncertainty and pain, one I was often on the losing side of.

I dabbled in trying to figure out if there would be a career better suited for my circumstances, but nothing stuck. Everything ended up being slimy sales that I wanted no part of, or internet scams trying to prey on people desperate for money and jobs.

Despite the setbacks and frustrations, I refused to lose hope, clinging to the belief that change was possible and that brighter days lay ahead. I had to hold onto hope, knowing that losing it would mean losing myself entirely, along with any chance of finding relief. Once someone gives in to the despair of a condition, it becomes incredibly difficult to recover because the darkness only compounds and feeds on itself, spiraling into deeper depths. And though the road ahead may be fraught with challenges, I faced it head-on, fueled by a newfound sense of determination and resilience.

Chapter 6

Surrendered Soul

As I struggled to navigate my journey alone, my marvelous mother stood unwavering in the background, a beacon of true hope and resilience. While I had resigned myself to the belief that medical intervention was futile, she tirelessly pursued alternative avenues in search of answers for my ever present affliction—Myoclonus Dystonia.

For nearly five years, I had avoided doctors and conventional treatments, convinced that there was no point in seeking further medical assistance. But my mother's determination knew no bounds, and she delved deep into research once again, uncovering a glimmer of hope in the form of unconventional therapies.

Amidst her tireless efforts, she stumbled upon the notion of spirit attachments as a potential cause for unexplained illnesses and addictions. Intrigued by the possibility of spiritual intervention, we jumped into a journey into the unknown, grasping at the promise of liberation from my afflictions.

Under the guidance of a remote spirit release therapist, we embarked on an unconventional treatment, clinging to the hope of a miraculous cure. Release therapists and energy workers capable of clearing a wide range of intrusive energies including spirit attachments, black magic, curses, dark energy and intrusive energy from other parts of the cosmos. Some unexplainable medical conditions have been shown to disappear after this type of treatment so I was willing to try the seemingly harmless treatment. Yet, as the process unfolded, the toll it exacted on my physical and emotional well-being became increasingly apparent.

I endured nights plagued by relentless nightmares, grappled with debilitating insomnia, and battled a myriad of physical, flu-like ailments that left me teetering on the brink of despair. Yet, in the depths of my suffering, I clung to the belief that liberation was within reach, a beacon of hope amidst the darkness. I clung onto hope as it seemed to be the only thing keeping me alive.

But as the weeks wore on and the treatment intensified, my resolve began to waver. Exhausted and overwhelmed, I found myself at a crossroads, teetering on the precipice of surrender. And in the early hours of April 27th, 2017, as I lay broken and depleted, I uttered a desperate prayer to a higher power, relinquishing control and surrendering to the unknown. I said with every essence of my being that I gave up, and that I could no longer do it alone.

In that moment of profound vulnerability, I experienced a shift—a seismic transformation that transcended the confines of the physical realm. The moment I surrendered with everything, ended up being the moment I experienced freedom and peace. It was like the weight of a thousand boulders and the stings of a hundred whips were ripped away from me as if they were nothing more than silk sheets. Millions of voices shouting from an angry crowd were silenced like they could no longer speak even a whisper. It was the calmest and most serene moment I had ever encountered in this tangible, three-dimensional world.

And then, in a voice that resonated with a clarity that defied comprehension, I heard the question that would alter the course of my life forever: "Are you ready?"

Without hesitation, I offered a resolute YES, embracing the unknown with unwavering resolve. And in the blink of an eye, I was released from the confines of my physical form, and propelled into a realm where the boundaries of reality blurred. I was Nowhere.

Chapter 7

A Glimpse Beyond Life's Edge

In this chapter, I won't delve into all of the remarkable events of my near-death experience, as I have extensively shared and discussed them elsewhere. Instead, I'll focus on highlighting some of the impactful experiences that have shaped the life I've led since that profound moment.

As soon as I left my body, I was pure energy, surrounded by pure energy in what looked like blackness. I was in this void, the absence of anywhere, anything, anyone, or any time. It was nowhere, no place, no-thing, no one, and no time. And yet, it was everything. It was filled with incomprehensible amounts of energy.

In this space, I met the Creator, God, Source. The energy that saved me from my earthly torture. I felt no judgment or sadness, only pure compassion and love. For a moment I had the realization that I wasn't where I had been and I asked, "Am I dead?" At the moment of this thought, three monks floated by with laugh-like grins as if to say, "If you only knew." It would be six more years before I grasped the meaning behind their smiles. Those smiles weren't about death or being dead; rather, they symbolized that there is no such thing as death, only a transition and a transfer of energy beyond the physical realm.

I was then traveling at what felt like warp speed through an amazing, bright blue, ethereal tunnel filled with 1s and 0s speeding past me so fast that they were almost just a blur. I also knew I was being downloaded with information. Much like the umbilical cord passes information and life unto an unborn child, I was being downloaded and filled with information and life of the universe. I wasn't conscious of the information, just of the importance of it.

Another integral aspect of my journey was the profound revelation of thought's creative force. Alongside fellow beings, I traversed a realm akin to Earth, where each fleeting thought birthed instant reality. This awe-inspiring phenomenon not only underscored the paramount significance of our thoughts but also magnified their staggering power.

I anticipate that further experiences beyond life's threshold will unfold as I progress through the human journey. However, as of this book, seven years following that pivotal experience, these are the two aspects that have drastically shaped my path.

Chapter 8

Whispers of Reprieve

When I found myself unexpectedly back in my body, feeling my heart beat again after an eight-minute lapse, I was convinced that if I opened my eyes, I would awaken inside a coffin buried six feet underground. The experience I had felt like weeks, not the mere eight minutes of earthly time that had passed.

Before daring to open my eyes, I desperately yearned to return to the place I had just come from. I attempted deep relaxation, meditative breaths, and even resorted to pleading. But nothing worked, and so I reluctantly opened my eyes, realizing only eight minutes had passed since I last looked at the clock before the ordeal. I had no clue what had just transpired, and the next four and a half years would be spent in a quest to unravel the mystery.

In addition to the time-bending event, I began to experience heightened metaphysical abilities unlike anything before. I could sense others' bodily pains and hear their thoughts. I felt disconnected from my own body, as if I were an oversized sausage crammed into a tight casing. The solidity of the world around me felt alien and foreign, like a visitor from a distant planet stranded on this unfamiliar, solid terrain. My mom sought out metaphysical therapists to help me comprehend the experience, but I remained bewildered and yearned to return to the place I had been on April 27th. I tried desperate measures to return, only finding myself further entangled in earthly troubles.

At the urging of my mom, I attended an International Association for Near-Death Studies (IANDS) event to meet others with extraordinary experiences. Despite being in denial and confusion, I went, hoping to find answers. I did connect with some other amazing individuals who shared about their own near-death experiences (NDEs) but I was lost and I was in an entirely new state of survival.

A year and a half after the early April morning event, I slowly realized I had no symptoms of Myoclonus Dystonia. This revelation unfolded cautiously for me. I shared my story for the first time on Jeff Mara's podcast titled, "Her Near Death Experience Cured Her Rare Disease!" I was nervous and still kept my NDE hidden from the world, but I thought Jeff's platform would be a safe space to explore this aspect of my life.

I was finally free from the monsters that plagued me for most of my life. There were no signs of dark paranormal activity or Myoclonus Dystonia. Perhaps, I could finally lead a normal life. Thinking I could return to my old career and my old hobbies with ease, I jumped right in. I returned to my old life, hopeful for a fresh start.

Chapter 9

Echos of the Past

With my past illness, encounters with dark entities, and tumultuous relationships behind me, I embarked on a journey to start anew. Returning to my career in marketing at a familiar company and settling back into my old home brought a sense of familiarity tinged with hope for a better future. I thought by returning to my old identity without the heavy dark aspects of my past, that I would be able to succeed and excel in my corporate life even faster and easier.

Initially, things seemed promising. Despite grappling with traumas resurfacing in familiar environments, I tackled them with resilience. Mild symptoms of Myoclonus Dystonia reappeared, but they didn't disrupt my life significantly, so I soldiered on, pouring my energy into both work and home life.

My efforts paid off when I was scouted by an amazing company on the East Coast, offering an opportunity in Georgia. Thrilled by the prospect, I relocated to Atlanta, signing a lease for a stunning apartment in the bustling heart of the city. It was a dream come true.

I reveled in the vibrant city life, my fulfilling job, and the bustling energy of my surroundings. But as I slipped back into my old identity, and my old actions, including the one of pushing myself relentlessly, Myoclonus Dystonia reared its head with newfound intensity. To add to my woes, I received a daunting cancer diagnosis just months after arriving.

Determined to tackle this new challenge head-on, my mom sent me Dr. Joe Dispenza's book, "You Are the Placebo" where he discusses how he healed his own broken back through meditation. As I fingered through his story, I thought, "so what," we've already tried dozens of holistic approaches without much success.

Just as I was navigating this tumultuous period, the fear of COVID-19 gripped the world, plunging us into lock-down. The fear of the unknown virus made receiving treatment for my known cancer nearly impossible. Surgeries were postponed unless it was an emergency and my condition was not deemed to be so. The once hopping office environment became isolated remote work.

Locked in my apartment, alone, with both illnesses, my focus shifted from fixing my health to mere survival.

Despite the setbacks, a glimmer of hope emerged when the cancer growth was successfully removed. This was a temporary ray of sunshine peeking through the still heavy storm. The battle with Myoclonus Dystonia persisted, and my spirits continued to wane.

Amidst the turmoil, I made another monumental decision—to find solace in gratitude. As the world grappled with despair, I sought out small blessings, acknowledging the beauty of flowers and nature's treasures scattered amidst the once bustling city streets. I knew I had to pull myself out of the darkness and I knew that gratitude would ease that, at least temporarily. With each moment of gratitude, my heart swelled, nurturing a newfound sense of resilience and appreciation for life's simple joys. I also found nature preserves scattered within the city, that my dog and I could enjoy as an escape from the once busy city streets. I would be grateful for them too. As I sought out more and more to be grateful for, the less I would need to try. My grateful heart began to grow. The more I fed it, the more self-sustaining it would become.

Chapter 10

Reluctant Retreat into Dependence

Despite the growing gratefulness in my heart, the hope of remaining in Atlanta and embracing independence was slowly slipping away. Companies were having major lay-offs including mine and I became without income. Seeking out other jobs was also difficult at the time as everyone was letting go of help and not bringing it on. Employment was at a low and my illness was at a high. With my finances dwindling, I faced the agonizing decision to return to Colorado. Going back meant I had failed at independence once again. It was a bitter pill to swallow, but I knew that staying in Atlanta would only lead me deeper into darkness and despair.

Back in Colorado, I tried to carry on the best I could. I poured my heart into work, self-medicated relentlessly, and attempted to nurture love in my life. But despite my efforts, everything seemed to crumble around me. My career faltered, my relationships soured, and my health deteriorated. Each day felt like a relentless test from the universe, and I couldn't help but feel like I was failing at every turn. Even the gratitude I had cultivated seemed to wither in the face of adversity.

Taking a sabbatical from work, I searched desperately for a glimmer of hope. Despite the worsening state of my health, I clung to gratitude and hope, though they seemed to slip through my fingers like grains of sand. Eventually, I reached a point where simple tasks became insurmountable challenges—I could no longer navigate stairs, apply makeup, or even button my clothes without assistance. Moving in with my mom felt like a temporary solution, but I feared there was no end in sight to my struggles.

In a stroke of luck—or perhaps divine intervention—my mom turned to social media support groups in search of answers. I had never imagined social media could be used for anything other than trivial chatter, but my mom wielded it as a powerful tool for research and connection. Through a support group, I was connected with a new doctor who offered a glimmer of hope in the form of brain surgery.

Despite the brain surgery being successful, it held a grim warning. Myoclonus Dystonia was considered an incredibly devious disorder where it would most likely learn its way around the deep brain stimulation system that the brain surgery had implanted. For the time being, it was exactly what I needed. The most profound outcome of the brain surgery was the newfound freedom from survival mode—a turning point in my life that marked the beginning of a new chapter.

Chapter 11

An Unexpected Detour

The surgery surpassed all expectations, leaving me nearly symptom-free once again. With a deep brain stimulator (DBS) implant delivering constant electrical pulses to the deep recesses of my brain, supplemented by medication that my body tolerated well, I felt invincible. Filled with boundless hope and gratitude, I returned to work sooner than advised, convinced that I could conquer anything. Once again, I pushed too hard and too fast and didn't allow time for healing.

Amidst this wave of positivity, I received a job offer for a position I hadn't even known existed in my field. The company, the location, and the recognition of my skills were a tremendous boost to my ego. I was not only valued but deeply wanted—a feeling that elevated my spirits to new heights. Excited to embark on this new journey, I eagerly accepted the offer.

Yet, amidst the excitement, the reality of my recent brain surgery and the lingering effects of past traumas loomed large. Despite my determination to excel in my new role, I knew deep down that I wasn't fully equipped to handle the demands it entailed. My mom, always guided by love and wisdom, gently urged me to reconsider.

Reluctantly, I acknowledged the truth in her words. Accepting the job would mean pushing myself beyond my limits and risking a setback in my recovery. With a heavy heart, I declined the offer—a decision that weighed heavily on my soul. For days, I agonized over the possibility of retracting my decision, but deep down, I knew it was the right choice.

Moving back in with my parents, I allowed myself to grieve for the path not taken. Yet, within the depths of my sorrow, I found solace in moments of introspection. Through a combination of exhaustion, self-hypnosis, and meditation, I found myself in this dimension and the one just beyond it simultaneously. It was reminiscent of the profound experience I had in 2017, but this time, I was fully present in both the physical world and the realm of endless energy.

In this state of introspection, I sought answers. I questioned whether I had made a mistake, where my path would lead from there, and what my purpose truly was. The answers I received guided me towards a new direction—to prioritize feeding my soul over feeding my ego. This revelation marked the beginning of a transformative journey, culminating in the creation of my first book—a testament to the power of embracing one's true calling.

Chapter 12

Unforeseen Remedies

A month after bidding farewell to my former corporate self, a remarkable transformation began to unfold. As I navigated the labyrinth of grief, shedding the layers of my past identity, I witnessed the intricate fabric of my being unraveling before me. But rather than fraying into disarray, the threads of my existence began to weave themselves anew, crafting a breathtaking mosaic from the remnants of my past.

I embarked on another new journey of self-discovery, penning stories that seemed disconnected and yet intricately intertwined. Embracing physical activities long abandoned, I reveled in the joy of exploration, liberated from the shackles of survival mode that had bound me for two decades. Exploring new hobbies, new possible career paths, and a new way of living had me chasing new possibilities like a child chasing the next seashell on an ever-changing beach.

Yet, beneath the surface, remnants of my former struggles persisted. Barely a month after the release of my second book, I found myself once again tethered to medical intervention, requiring additional programming for my DBS unit to quell resurging symptoms. I was reminded how Myoclonus Dystonia is a cunning condition and usually finds a way around any interventions. The only option was to add more energy to the system. The hum of electricity surged through my brain.

Despite my newfound liberation, subconscious programs ingrained over two decades lingered, their presence a subtle reminder of past battles. Entrusting my physical well-being to a team of capable doctors, I turned inward, starting on a quest to rewrite the programs that had been etched deep within my psyche in states of survival.

Through serendipitous encounters orchestrated by the cosmos, I found a guide, a coach—a beacon of light amidst the shadows. With her guidance, I paved a path leading into the depths of my subconscious, unraveling layers of conditioning that no longer served me. Forging a path toward self-discovery and empowerment, I embraced vulnerability, and acknowledged my need for support.

As discussions unfolded, the notion of a meditation retreat emerged—a transformative journey into the realm beyond the senses. Doubt did enter my mind, would this holistic approach prove any more successful then past attempts? Having no real income also had me questioning if I should spend so much money on a mere possibility. Though initially hesitant, I seized the opportunity, immersing myself in preparations for the profound experience that lay ahead. I had never studied or practiced this type of meditation, only being familiar with mindfulness meditations from the past. This method of leaving the body and the 3D senses was very new to me and there were prerequisites I had to complete before the retreat. With determination as my guide, I ventured on a pilgrimage of the soul, venturing into the unknown depths of consciousness.

This meditation was unlike any I had encountered before—an odyssey through the realms of the mind, a voyage into the boundless expanse of the soul. Guided by the teachings of Dr. Joe Dispenza, whose wisdom I had once dismissed in a prior state of survival, I embarked on a pilgrimage of self-discovery, ready to embrace the infinite possibilities that awaited.

Chapter 13

The First Creation

As I drove over the majestic mountains toward the Denver retreat, excitement pulsed through my veins. In a huge leap of faith, I made the journey; even though I wasn't sure what my odds were of getting into the event without a confirmed spot. Immersed in the intensive and progressive course, I marveled at the serendipity of it all. Despite the odds stacked against me, I booked a hotel room for the night, hopeful for a chance to participate in the sold-out event.

Arriving at the bustling conference center at the Gaylord, I eagerly joined the walk-in wait list, fueled by anticipation. I was early but already 30th or so, in line to do the same thing. I signed-up on the wait list, and I was told I would receive an email if I came off and could then proceed in buying a ticket. I then headed to a local neighborhood park. It was July so it was sunny and beautiful.

I didn't have much cell service which is not uncommon for that area of Denver. As I soaked up the warm July sun in a tranquil neighborhood park, I delved into the pages of "Becoming Supernatural," learning more about the hows and the whys to meditate, immersing myself in the science behind spirituality.

Alone amidst the soothing melodies of nature, I was immersed in meditation, surrendering to the depths of my consciousness. A type of meditation I had been unfamiliar with just a few weeks prior. Covered in a blanket of peace and tranquility, I savored the euphoria of the moment, basking in the radiant glow of the sun. I had a roll-out beach blanket with a built in pillow that I keep in my car in case of sun-soaking emergencies. It was perfect for the occasion. I attempted breathwork and disappeared into the blackness even though the sun was bright and should have been lighting up my eyelids. It was an incredible feeling and I was once again filled with peace and serenity. When I opened my eyes I was elated and filled with excitement. It was time to check into my hotel.

Filled with renewed vigor, I checked into my hotel, brimming with excitement for what lay ahead. Despite a fleeting moment of doubt upon checking my email, I resolved to maintain a positive mindset. I showered and put on a beautiful and deceivingly comfortable dress. I checked my email once again and nothing. I checked my two email folders and their spam folders realizing I signed up using the wrong email.

Then the nerves hit. Oh no, I used the wrong email to check in and they won't know that I completed the pre-requisites. What happens if I don't get in? Then, as my nerves were ramping up and the familiar "what if" doom spiral started, I thought about waiting at a nearby bar so I could have a drink to calm my nerves while I waited.

That's when it hit me that I needed a different way of thinking. I decided to go back to the conference center and be in the powerful energy of eager participants while I waited, instead of waiting at a bar. I had also been cramming the Intensive and Progressive Program as well as reading through "Becoming Supernatural" and in those materials, I knew what to do. I would do exactly what Dr. Joe was teaching through his works to get me into his retreat.

Shaking off the nerves, I decided to immerse myself in the energy of the conference center, channeling the teachings of Dr. Joe Dispenza.

With unwavering determination, I visualized my entrance into the retreat, embracing the transformative power of intention. Fueled by anticipation, I awaited the long-awaited email, my heart pounding with excitement.

I closed my eyes, took a deep breath, and knew that when I opened my eyes and opened the door, that I would be stepping out of my hotel room, and into the room of the retreat. And I stayed in that energy the whole drive there which was about 20 minutes. I held onto it further while I sat in the hallway refreshing my emails over and over until the nerves started to hit again. What if...

I once again thought to myself, nope, we are not doing that and with that I stood up. I went to speak with a gentleman I met earlier, who was volunteering. He looked at me and said, "You finally got your ticket?" with authentic enthusiasm to which I replied that I had not. He shook his head in confusion saying they had sent out emails and that I should go check with the walk-in volunteer. So of course, I went over to where she was sitting and when I asked her about the email she snarkingly said she had sent me one and asked if I had checked my junk mail. Um, yes, many times is what I thought to myself, but I politely simply said that I had. She said she would send it again and then there it was!

I started the process of buying the ticket and the registration doors were starting to close. This was the longest ticket form I had ever seen! It felt like I was trying to read a novel and answer questions while at the same time running in what felt like slow motion to the registration doors that were closing. When I reflect on this memory, I understand that my mind has convinced me it was all very dramatic. In reality, it all happened in a reasonable amount of 3D physical time. But it is so much more fun to see the dramatic version. Flying slow-motion across a giant hallway as the doors are closing to my future. The replay in my mind replays it as if those doors had closed, then I wouldn't have gotten in, when in reality everyone was very kind and very patient.

As soon as I entered the registration doors, no one seemed to be in a rush. So I skimmed the questions answering in the way I thought wouldn't cause any extra trouble and bought my ticket.

With determination as my guide, I secured my ticket, a tangible symbol of my journey into the unknown. I then got a name tag where they wrote my name down and I ran to pick my group color for the week. I picked blue for two reasons. The first reason being that the gentlemen I met twice that day who had helped me was in the blue group and told me I should try to get in his group. The second reason being blue has been my favorite color since my near-death experience in 2017.

Adorned with a vibrant blue name tag, I reveled in the thrill of accomplishment, my heart brimming with joy. I was in, I was excited, I was elated, and in partial disbelief. I sat down next to a young girl and she looked at my name tag and said, "Oh, you're one of those people." I would later find out that people who manage to get into the sold out events are a rarity and usually are talked about among the crowd of people.

Chapter 14

Discovering the Keys Within

Unable to sleep, a blend of excitement and nervousness kept me restless. Having been out of work for nine months and relying on my savings and family's support during my healing journey from brain surgery, I felt a mix of emotions as I dove into this transformative retreat.

Morning arrived, and I anticipated a peaceful meditation session, only to find myself struggling to quiet my mind. Disappointed by my initial attempts, I resolved to let go and embrace the present moment.

After a rejuvenating breakfast outside in the bright July sun, I returned to the auditorium for more sessions, each blending into the next in a whirlwind of enlightenment. Dr. Joe Dispenza's teachings on the science of spirituality, and meditation, resonated deeply with me, offering profound insights into the body's innate capacity for healing.

If you are unfamiliar with Dr. Joe Dispenza and his work, he teaches a lot about the science of spirituality, or the science of meditation. What is actually going on in the body and why that allows for healing. He also explains what is going on in the universe and the quantum and how we can create our reality with that. In his meditations, along with many other types practiced around the world and in other cultures and religions, something beautiful happens in the body. The heart and the brain go into coherence and when they are in coherence together, the brain and the body work together to promote health, healing, and order. Dr. Joe and the researchers at the Inner Science Research Fund have been able to see both the body and the heart in coherence using technology. Evidence of this experience is marked by the heart beating in a different way, a new way that creates beautiful geometric patterns. They can also match the heart waves to the coherent brain waves that they read through electroencephalogram (EEG) machines.

During one particularly profound meditation, I transcended my physical senses and entered a realm of darkness reminiscent of my near-death experience. In this ethereal space, I witnessed the synchronicity of my heart and brain, their harmonious coherence a testament to the power of meditation. I saw my heart and my brain organs appear from the darkness and communicate as one in harmony.

Suddenly, fragments of my near-death experience tunnel emerged from the darkness, weaving through my heart and brain in perfect harmony. This code was coming in from my 8th energy center into my heart, where it was washed with love and gratitude before making its way into my brain. This process of receiving code from nowhere and it entering through my heart and into my brain went on for an indefinite amount of time, as I just noticed it all in awe. It was as though this divine code was rewriting the very fabric of my being, ushering in a profound transformation.

In a moment of profound clarity within the meditation, I realized that this experience had not only healed my past programs but also rewired the neural pathways associated with Myoclonus Dystonia. Despite not seeking a cure for my disorder, the profound healing I experienced was beyond anything I could have imagined. The joyous side effect of that experience was that it also rewired the parts of my brain that created the disorder, Myoclonus Dystonia.

Filled with newfound faith from an overwhelming sense of knowing that stemmed from both the meditation and the understanding of how others had also spontaneously healed, I made a bold decision to turn off my Deep Brain Stimulation (DBS) system. I carried a controller for the unit almost everywhere I went in case I needed to adjust a setting because I was getting into symptom trouble. So, of course it was with me at this retreat, along with my 5 different medications I was still taking. Despite the initial fear and uncertainty of turning off the stimulator, I trusted in the healing power within me.

I ended up sleeping great through the night and returned to the retreat on the Fourth of July. This is a big day in the United States and people all over the country, regardless of political views, come and celebrate Independence Day together. At 10:02 in the morning, I decided to turn off the DBS system. It was a little terrifying. I had never turned it off before, what would happen if I needed to turn it back on and I couldn't? Also, I could tell a difference in my body within minutes of even the slightest adjustment to the settings - what would happen if I just completely shut it off?

That's where faith came into play. I not only knew that I could heal but I believed I did. During a break, I was sitting near the back of the auditorium and I went through the motions. I connected the computer that was in my chest to my "router" which then connected to my controller which was really just a cell phone with 1 program on it. The whole connection process took less than two minutes, which was common as I often connected to the device to tweak my settings. The program that was keeping my brain in check for 17 months now. The device that I had waited 12 years to try out. The neuro-stimulator that was more successful than the doctors even hoped. And there I was, shutting it off..

I clicked on a button I had never clicked on before "Turn Off Device." Both fear and excitement arose as I clicked the button, then another appeared as a warning, confirming I wanted to turn off the device. As I disconnected the device, a wave of anticipation swept over me. Every sensation, every movement, was met with a mix of apprehension and excitement. With each passing moment, I felt a profound shift within me, a deep sense of healing and renewal taking root.

Days passed, and the undeniable truth of my healing journey became evident. Each second, each minute and each day went on without a twitch, without a tremor, without a twinge of pain, without an intrusive thought. With each moment, I embraced the newfound freedom and vitality coursing through my veins.

Finally, on that fateful Friday, I shared my journey with others, confident in the miraculous transformation that had taken place within me. In that moment, I knew with every fiber of my being that I was healed once again.

Chapter 15

Retrospective Clarity

Now, we delve into the heart of the story, the very essence that compelled me to type these words. The journey of healing that unfolded before me, revealing profound revelations and unlocking the keys to my transformation.

First and foremost, let's dispel any notion that my ability to heal stemmed from being an advanced meditator. Far from it. Just a week prior to my breakthrough, I had barely scratched the surface of meditation. The specific techniques or meditations used are inconsequential; what truly mattered was the profound inner work I had undertaken beforehand with the combination of the spiritual work of meditation.

Enter the realm of shadow work. For those unfamiliar with the term, your shadow is essentially the wounded part of you. I didn't know what this term was until well after the retreat. I had spent decades innately working on healing the parts of me that were hurt and damaged. The traumas, the low self-esteem, the lack of self-worth, and the events that damaged both my ego and my soul. I had done years of hypnosis to try to work on my subconscious wounds, I did Eye Movement Desensitization and Reprocessing (EMDR) to work on my conscious wounds and triggers that would instantly put me back into fight, flight, and freeze modes, and most importantly, I worked on forgiveness. Not just forgiveness of others who had hurt me, but forgiveness of myself. After I learned that I could forgive without forgetting, and remembering the past without the pain, I learned how to forgive myself. Whether or not those traumas were my fault or not, I had to forgive myself for whatever role I thought I played in them.

I had to cut ties to that past identity and those past feelings of not being understood and the identity that brought pain. For example, victims of abuse often end up in abuse cycles, not because they want to, or even feel like they deserve it, but because they are so terrified of it happening again that they inadvertently create that reality. The thought of it happening again creates the potential and with fear being such a strong emotion, it acts like a magnet and draws it into reality. There's a saying "what you resist, persits." I learned that it is possible to create a reality through thoughts and emotions, but in order to create a happy, healthy reality, you must be detached from the negative, fear and anger based feelings. Looking back, I had done a lot of this work without even realizing the full potential it would bring me.

It was imperative to sever ties with my past identity, relinquishing the role of being a person with Myoclonus Dystonia and not being understood along with embracing a mindset of empowerment. By releasing the grip of fear and anger, I unlocked the potential to shape my reality with intention and purpose.

But the journey didn't stop there. I started on yet another quest to cultivate a heart overflowing with gratitude. Through the darkest of days, I nurtured a spirit of thankfulness, finding solace in the simplest of joys. With each act of gratitude, my soul ignited with newfound vigor, immune to the negativity that once clouded my existence. The more I made it a conscious effort to be grateful, the less I needed to. It was like an infection that was resistant to negativity and naysayers. Once my heart filled completely with gratitude, there was nothing that could take that away.

Gratitude, I discovered, is a potent elixir for healing, transcending limitations and ushering in a wave of transformation. It is independent of an end result and independent of others. Gratitude is an emotion of the soul and the more you strengthen the muscle, the easier it is to break into the possibility of healing. A grateful heart doesn't want, because it does not perceive a sense of lack; it is consumed with what it already has. The feeling of being in lack slows down your energy and frequency, making it both much more difficult to create reality as well increasing the time it takes for it to happen. Gratitude is an elevated emotion lending itself to create faster and easier. Finding and filling my grateful heart was another side to shadow work that I had worked really hard at. In that shadow work, gratitude became a spark of light.

When the journey with Myoclonus Dystonia began again, after the profound near-death experience that miraculously led to the initial healing of the condition, I was temporarily disheartened. Despite the initial triumph of the miraculous healing, the disorder reappeared later on, leaving me feeling like a failure and a fraud. This unexpected turn of events was a temporary setback that would ultimately play a crucial role in my journey towards permanent healing.

The recurrence of the condition triggered another period of deep reflection and introspection. I realized that the disorder's return was not a setback but rather another opportunity for growth and understanding. It forced me to recognize and confront the deeper underlying issues that contributed to its re-manifestation in the first place.

Through this process, I gained invaluable insights into the interconnected nature of mind, body, and spirit in the healing process. The relationship between the body, mind, and soul is a philosophical and spiritual topic that has been discussed by many different cultures and belief systems throughout history. Generally, it is believed that the body, mind, and soul are interconnected and influence one another. This symbiotic relationship posits that the body, mind, and soul are not disparate entities but rather intertwined aspects that profoundly influence one another.

The body serves as the tangible vessel housing our existence, intimately connected to our sensory perceptions like touch, taste, and sight. Meanwhile, the mind acts as the hub of consciousness, housing our cognitive faculties such as memory, reasoning, and perception. Beyond these corporeal and cognitive realms, the soul emerges as the ethereal essence of our being, often conceptualized as the eternal and spiritual core of our existence.

Varied belief systems offer nuanced perspectives on the soul's role, with some viewing it as the immutable true self transcending the body and mind. Conversely, others perceive the soul as intricately intertwined with the body and mind, shaping our emotions, desires, and motivations. Some believe that the soul is the source of our consciousness and that it is what gives us our unique sense of identity.

The relationship between the body, mind, and soul is often seen as a holistic one, in which all three are interconnected and interdependent. In this view, optimal health and well-being are achieved when all three are in balance and harmony with one another. This can be achieved through practices such as meditation, yoga, and other forms of mindfulness that integrate the body, mind, and soul. I learned that true healing goes beyond mere physical symptoms and requires addressing emotional, psychological, and spiritual imbalances as well.

Moreover, the experience of healing, relapse, and subsequent recovery taught me important lessons about resilience, perseverance, and self-compassion. It challenged me to cultivate a deeper sense of self-awareness and to adopt more powerful lifestyle practices that supported my overall well-being.

In hindsight, I now recognize that the recurrence of Myoclonus Dystonia was a necessary part of my healing journey. It provided me with the opportunity to delve deeper into the root causes of the condition and to develop more sustainable and effective healing strategies for not only myself, but for others as well.

Ultimately, this journey from initial healing to relapse to permanent recovery was a transformative one that reshaped my understanding of health and healing. It taught me the importance of holistic approaches to wellness and the power of resilience in overcoming life's challenges. Learning more about the mind, body and soul connection, I was able to learn just how important and powerful each of these parts to the whole is. By learning how to harness the power of each and combine them, anything is possible.

After understanding more about how thoughts, feelings, and actions are directly responsible for our reality, I was able to understand why, and how, my condition came back. Healers of both the past and the present, after healing someone, will tell them to change their lives, not to go back to their old ways. The body is so subjective that once someone returns to their old thoughts, their old feelings, their old actions, and their old identities, that the body believes it is still living in the past. What also exists in the past? The condition in which they were healed of, and it gets recreated. Some healers also tell the person not to speak of the healing for the energies of doubt and disbelief are infectious and can also cause the person to return to their previous state of being.

I say all of this because I was unaware of it all. I was healed from my near-death experience, but I didn't

know any better so I returned to my old way of thinking, feeling and doing. I returned to my past identity and
in my past identity, laid my condition. My body didn't
know any better and recreated the illness of my past
because nothing had changed. I don't blame myself for
it returning because I didn't have the knowledge or the
language to do otherwise. In my studies since, I have
not only learned the language of how to get back to the
"Nowhere" filled with limitless possibilities, but also the
language of how to continue to create a new identity and
not slip back into my old one.

A profound truth emerged throughout this process.
My journey wasn't just about personal healing; it was a
call to empower others on their path to self-discovery.
By embracing my role as a catalyst for transformation, I
stepped into the realm of divine healing, offering guidance and support to those seeking their own path to
wellness.

In the grand puzzle of life, miracles are not mere
happenstance; they are the result of our collective understanding and evolution. Through this journey of self-
discovery, I have come to realize that miracles are simply
phenomena we have yet to fully comprehend. And it is
through this understanding that we unlock the limitless
potential of our own divine healing.

Chapter 16

Practical Strategies for Breaking Free

Let's embark on a journey through the lessons garnered from 22 years of profound exploration, aimed at unveiling the divine powers of healing within you. This chapter is your guide, offering invaluable insights into unleashing your inner strength and embracing a future filled with possibility.

The foremost lesson, and perhaps the most pivotal, centers around the incredible power of our thoughts. It's a notion often reiterated - the importance of mindfulness in our thoughts and words. The experience of thoughts instantly manifesting in my NDE experience gave me great insight into our world. It showed me that thoughts do create our reality. It also gave me gratitude that we have time to change our thoughts before they manifest, unlike in my experience. Thoughts are an extremely powerful tool of creation. Yet, how deeply have we delved into this concept? Have we truly grasped its magnitude? If you've ever found yourself striving for positivity with little to show for it, perhaps there's more beneath the surface.

Breaking free from the shackles of victim-hood is another crucial step on this transformative journey. Whether it's battling illness, overcoming abuse, or navigating the complexities of conventional medicine, shedding the victim mentality unveils a world of untapped potential. It's a paradigm shift, realizing that life isn't happening to you, but for you. If you're ready to break free from this mindset, tools and resources abound to guide you. Exploring pre-birth plans and soul contracts, or recognizing recurring patterns in your life, can offer invaluable insights. At age 17, before I was even diagnosed, my mom had the insight that we had signed up for this soul contract together. She realized she had her own lessons she was supposed to learn through our shared experience. The painful journey we both had to go on has uncovered both of our spiritual gifts and insights. A bittersweet journey, but a beautiful necessity for our ultimate growth and understanding.

Sometimes we aren't even aware that we have the victim mindset. In this case, you can look for patterns that have repeated in your life. Abusive relationships regardless of a new partner, medical mistreatment despite vetting new doctors, repeated sexual abuse despite taking all the precautions, and other patterns that you may see playing out in your life. This could be due to a victim mindset or a soul lesson you need to become aware of. Another way to recognize this mindset is if you find yourself asking, "Why did God let this happen?" or, "Why me?"

Emotional beliefs often accompany the victim-hood mindset, manifesting as low self-confidence and diminished self-worth. These emotional barriers can hinder healing progress, creating a barrier between you and your innate potential for healing.

Transitioning from survival-mode emotions to elevated states of being is key to unlocking your healing journey. Emotions rooted in survival, such as fear, anger, and shame, exert a powerful influence on our well-being. By embracing higher emotions like willingness, joy, and gratitude, you pave the way for profound healing and transformation. While I had never really experienced a healthy body due to the Myoclonus Dystonia or the survival mode that my near-death experience put me in, I had lots of experiences with joy and gratitude. Our imagination is so strong that if we are able to think of a reality and assign a familiar emotion to it, we can create it.

Some of the survival emotions include self-loathing, self-hatred, anger towards others, regrets, blame and shame. Maybe you did some things out of survival that you aren't proud of and this creates anxiety when you think of your past, perhaps you even hate yourself for those occurrences. There could also be anger and hatred for others. Whether it be because someone else's actions caused your condition or someone wasn't there in the way you needed them to be. Fear is another powerful emotion, but it is powerful in that it is unconducive of healing. These lower energies will keep you stuck. Negative and low feelings and emotions often get trapped in your survival centers. These centers are located in your pelvis and stomach. Some people know them as chakras.

I'm going to share the fastest way of breaking free from all of the low de-elevated emotions such as worry, fear, shame, guilt, anger, lust and start feeling and embracing the higher elevated emotions where you can begin to heal. These higher emotions consist of willingness, joy, peace, love, acceptance and most importantly, gratitude. Remember what I said about a grateful heart? It is independent of results and fills with things and experiences it already has. A fully grateful heart is a heart full of creation.

To break free from low emotions and survival reactions that happen as a response, I have found a few tools to help. If you find yourself in a survival response that seems to be escalating, try one of these mindfulness techniques to quickly get your mind and body back into the present moment and out of the past response. Step away to wash your hands and focus on the water rushing over them, smell the fragrance of the soap and listen to the bubbles pop as you move your hands together. If you are able to do 15 jumping jacks or run up a few flights of stairs, this will also help get you out of the survival mode response.

Once you have de-escalated the survival response, you can train your brain away from them using EFT/TFT Tapping protocols. EFT or the Emotional Freedom Technique draws on the ancient Chinese practice of acupuncture, which teaches that the body's energy travels along specific pathways. Certain points on these pathways are stimulated to improve the flow of energy. This can change the negative energy and survival response by allowing it to flow instead of build up. TFT or Thought Freedom Therapy expands on the EFT technique by using a combination of sight, sound, and tapping to rewire the brain. I am certified in both of these techniques and often work with my clients to utilize them. There are also plenty of resources on these techniques floating around on the internet, so the information is relatively easy to come by.

Hypnosis and guided meditations are other great resources for cutting ties with past emotions and thoughts. There are hundreds, if not thousands, of free hypnosis and guided meditation videos on YouTube for healing past traumas and cutting ties with them. With these resources being some of the most beneficial to me, I decided to also get certified in the processes to help my clients. Of course, there are also amazing hypnotists and therapists who can also help with this venture. The same goes for body-work. Yoga and somatic movements have also been shown to help the body let go of the stored traumas and release the blockages built up in the survival centers of the body. You can also find free videos to follow along with online or reach out to a trusted professional if you are called to this path of resolution.

Alongside these other freedom techniques, you can start to build your heart of gratitude. If you already have a gratitude practice, there is only more power building upon it. If you struggle with being grateful in the midst of a chronic illness, depression, or a painful event, start small. When I lost my ability to draw, which was my self-care throughout highschool, I adapted and started to paint. While I wasn't a fine art painter, I was still grateful I had an artistic outlook. When the world shut down due to a global scare, I was grateful that there were beautiful flowers at my apartment building. When my condition progressed to the point I was no longer independent, I was grateful I had a loving family who was willing to step in to help. You can find gratitude in every situation if you look hard enough and just like a muscle, the more you use it, the stronger it becomes. If you struggle with this aspect, there are lovely gratitude journals with prompts that can help you build that muscle.

Embarking on a journey of gratitude further accelerates your healing trajectory. Even amidst the darkest of times, gratitude serves as a beacon of light, illuminating the path forward. By cultivating external and internal gratitude, you forge a deeper connection with yourself and the world around you.

Once you have conquered the external gratitude, the internal gratefulness is the next mission. This is where you will start to heal some of the negative feelings and beliefs about yourself. Start recognizing all the things you are grateful for about yourself. Are you grateful that you are a patient person? Are you grateful that you have resilience or compassion? Find the characteristics about yourself that you are proud of and thank yourself for having them. Thank yourself for adopting these traits while in the midst of survival. There is no point in dwelling on the parts of you that you aren't so fond of in this exercise. Start being grateful for what makes you, you.

If you are amongst the majority of people who struggle with internal gratitude, there are a few tools you can utilize to get the thoughts and feelings flowing. The easiest may be asking a friend, loved one, or coworker what they admire about you. Another idea is to look at some aspects of yourself that may be positive attributes but can have negative consequences such as pushing yourself really hard. That is beneficial for resilience, getting things done, and moving forward but it can lead to burn out, fatigue, chronic stress and high cortisol. Keep a running tab on the positive parts of you even if they have some negative consequences. Accepting the negative consequences become a part of the self-forgiveness and self-compassion side of shadow work.

Another tool for cultivating self-compassion and inner gratitude is by looking at your past that has been filled with so many challenges, it's like a mountain. A mountain you overcame. Don't compare your mountain with others, just focus on your own. Focus on the paths you took, the gear you used, and how you, despite the odds or difficulties, were able to to get to where you are now.

All of these tools just mentioned help you cut ties with your past identity, your past personality, your past self. Breaking free from your past identity is paramount in shaping your future. Creating a new personality, and a new identity doesn't change who you are at the core, who you are on a soul level. By changing your responses to triggers and embracing transformative actions, you release the hold of the past, and are able to step into a future brimming with possibility while keeping your authentic self in the new, healthy identity.

Another way of cutting ties to the past self is by changing your actions. Changing your response to triggers is a major tool in creating a new future. Does a certain place, person, or phrase send your mind into a seemingly endless series of "What ifs?" and, "Oh nos?" When you are able to recognize that you are entering the cycle of fear and worry of the past, acknowledge that was a part of your past self and assure yourself that it is not a part of your present or your future. Ask yourself how repeating the old survival response will help you create the future you.

Evaluate your surroundings and make necessary changes to align with your healing journey. Whether it's altering your environment, cultivating supportive relationships, or reassessing your life's trajectory, every step you take brings you closer to embodying your divine healing potential.

I gave one of my clients this piece of advice after watching my sister do this throughout her life.

You are a beautiful flower trying to blossom in a garden of your life. When your garden is filled with other flowers trying to do the same, you all support each other in achieving health, beauty and vitality. When you are surrounded by weeds, they suck your energy and your strength from underneath you at your roots. No matter how much you try to share your optimism, beauty and health with them, they can't accept and will continue to steal your energy from underneath you. Weed your garden, take care of you and the other flowers on the same mission that you are on.

In essence, this chapter serves as a foundation for your transformational journey. It's a testament to the resilience of the human spirit and the boundless potential within each of us to heal, grow, and thrive. As you navigate through these strategies, remember that you hold the power to rewrite your story and embrace a future filled with vitality, purpose, and joy.

Chapter 17

Embody Your Power to Shape Reality

Now that you've taken bold steps to liberate yourself from the constraints of your past, shedding the dense emotions that once held you back, it's time to embark on a journey of creation. You stand at the threshold of a new reality, ready to craft a narrative that aligns with your deepest desires and aspirations.

In this exhilarating chapter, we delve into the transformative power of your thoughts and language, the potent keys that unlock the boundless potential within you for healing and growth.

First and foremost, let's explore the dynamic realm of NLP (Neuro-Linguistic Programming), a groundbreaking therapeutic approach that taps into the intricate interplay between language patterns, internal thought processes, and behavioral outcomes. Through NLP techniques like reframing and cognitive restructuring, you'll uncover the profound impact of language on your emotional landscape and personal development journey. By harnessing the power of NLP, you'll embark on a transformative journey of self-discovery and empowerment, paving the way for profound healing and growth.

Imagine a person who has experienced a setback at work and is feeling discouraged. Through reframing, they can shift their perspective from seeing the setback as a failure to viewing it as an opportunity for learning and growth. They might reframe their thoughts from "I failed at this task" to "This experience has taught me valuable lessons that will help me succeed in the future." This improves attitude, resilience, and motivation to learn through hardship.

Now consider someone struggling with anxiety about an upcoming social event. Through cognitive restructuring, they can challenge and modify their negative thought patterns. For instance, they might initially think, "I'll embarrass myself in front of everyone." With cognitive restructuring, they can reevaluate this thought, finding evidence to counter it such as recalling past successful social interactions or reminding themselves that everyone experiences nerves sometimes. This process helps them replace the negative thought with a more realistic and constructive one, like, "I've handled social situations well before, and I can do it again."

NLP techniques can empower individuals to reframe their perspectives and restructure their thoughts, leading to positive shifts in emotions and behaviors. Understanding the importance of internal and external language in everyday life as well as in the realm of healing, I have also undergone training to incorporate this modality into my life and the lives of my clients.

If you're drawn to the expressive realm of art, I suggest looking into the relatively new form of art therapy called Neurographia. Neurographia is a therapeutic approach that combines elements of drawing, mindfulness, and neuroscience to help individuals process emotions, release trauma, and promote healing. Developed by Russian artist and psychologist Pavel Piskarev, Neurographia utilizes specific drawing techniques and principles based on neuroplasticity to rewire neural pathways in the brain and facilitate emotional and physical healing. Neurographia provides a creative outlet for individuals to express and release pent-up emotions, traumas, and stressors through art. By channeling emotions into the drawing process, individuals can externalize their inner experiences and gain a deeper understanding of their emotions. Also, by engaging in Neurographia one can focus on the present moment and the act of drawing, which promotes mindfulness and relaxation. The repetitive and rhythmic nature of drawing can induce a meditative state, reducing stress and promoting a sense of calm and well-being.

My favorite part about this type of artwork is how it utilizes neuroplasticity. Neurographia leverages the principles of neuroplasticity, the brain's ability to reorganize and form new neural connections in response to experience. This also allows the brain to make repairs on damaged areas and networks of the brain. Through specific drawing techniques, individuals can stimulate neural pathways associated with positive emotions, resilience, and healing, thereby rewiring the brain for healing and overall well-being.

Neurographia can be particularly beneficial for individuals who have experienced trauma. The process of creating art allows individuals to externalize and process traumatic memories in a safe and nonverbal manner. By visually representing their experiences on paper, individuals can gain a sense of control over their trauma and begin to integrate and heal from it. This can be utilized in addition to some other trauma release methods mentioned earlier. Neurographia can also be a way of engaging in self-exploration and introspection as individuals engage in the drawing process. By reflecting on their drawings and the emotions they evoke, individuals can gain insight into their inner world, uncover subconscious patterns, and foster personal growth and self-awareness. Overall, Neurographia offers a unique and creative approach to healing that integrates art, mindfulness, and neuroscience principles. It provides individuals with a powerful tool for processing emotions, releasing trauma, and promoting holistic well-being. You can use this as a powerful resource should you find yourself stuck in an emotion. While not certified, I have studied the matter and put it into practice in my own life in order to better assist my clients.

Let's explore more on how your thoughts and your language create your reality. We've already explored some on how negative thoughts recreate traumas so now I want to focus on what the positive ones can do. Positive thoughts and positive language can influence someone's reality through various psychological and cognitive mechanisms. Positive thoughts and beliefs can shape one's expectations and perceptions of reality. When someone consistently thinks positively and believes in their abilities, they are more likely to approach challenges with confidence and optimism. This positive mindset can increase the likelihood of success and reinforce the belief that positive outcomes are possible, thus creating a self-fulfilling prophecy.

The brain has the remarkable ability to reorganize itself in response to experiences and thoughts, a phenomenon known as neuroplasticity. When someone consistently engages in positive thinking, it can lead to the strengthening of neural pathways associated with positive emotions, resilience, and well-being. Over time, this rewiring of the brain can result in a more positive outlook on life and a greater capacity to perceive and create positive experiences. We explored this concept in a past chapter when discussing how the brain is subjective and if you feel the old emotions and think the old thoughts, the brain believes it is living in that old reality and creates the old condition.

Habits are physically hardwired into the brain, both good ones and the bad ones. Imagine habits as a river that takes the path of least resistance. During heavy rainfall, the water will choose the route that is already there. It takes a lot of work to build a new habit or to build a new path and even harder when there is a downpour and the water tries to continue down the old, carved path of least resistance. This also happens in the brain through neural pathways. This process explains why it is often both hard and uncomfortable to break old habits as well as develop new ones.

As we delve deeper into the realm of thoughts and language, let's illuminate the transformative potential of positive thinking and affirmations. By cultivating a mindset rooted in optimism and self-belief, you'll harness the extraordinary power of neuroplasticity to rewire your brain and shape your reality. Through the practice of positive affirmations and visualizations, you'll amplify your healing journey, manifesting your deepest desires with unwavering clarity and conviction.

The Law of Attraction suggests that like attracts like, meaning that positive thoughts and energy can attract positive experiences into one's life. When someone focuses on positive thoughts and visualizes their desired outcomes, they are more likely to notice and seize opportunities that align with their intentions. This can lead to a reality characterized by abundance, success, and fulfillment. When you focus on positive thoughts and outcomes, you will tend to see more of it. It's a lot like confirmation bias where you find the evidence that best supports your point of view and disregards that which doesn't. In this case, it is conducive to healing.

On the flip-side, The Law of Attraction also holds true with the saying, "What you resist, persists." The more fearful you are of something happening, the more likely you are to draw it into reality.

I would like to include an example that I helped my mom work through. She wasn't in the mood to go for a hike but the dogs were relentless and insistent. My mom decided she would drive far into the public land away from people so that she could set up her paints and let the dogs run around without worrying about running into anyone. As she continued to drive further away from the towns, she would keep coming upon cars of people also wanting to get away from civilization. Each new car she spotted filled her with more fear about running into people and how she did not want to wrestle with the dogs. Alas, a spot free from vehicles and people emerged deep into the countryside. The dogs were let out and they began playing around her Jeep and as she was setting up, a man on a bicycle approached. Instead of riding around to the path, he instead had the need to blame my mom for parking where she did with a rather unsettling demeanor. Here she drove for over an hour with the sole purpose of not running into anyone unpleasant and merely minutes after arriving, that very thing happened.

We have since crafted a new narrative for when she wants to take the dogs on a walk in the countryside. The new thought process is an attitude of encountering people full of love for dogs and excitement for the shared outdoors. Since this change of narrative, she can now take the dogs just mere minutes away and not encounter anyone.

The Law of Attraction serves as a guiding principle in this transformative process, illuminating the profound connection between your thoughts, beliefs, and external reality. By aligning your thoughts and intentions with positive outcomes, you'll magnetize health, abundance, success, and fulfillment into your life. Embrace the infinite possibilities of the Law of Attraction as you cultivate a reality characterized by joy, prosperity, and boundless potential.

Maintaining a radiant and uplifting attitude amidst environments where negativity seems to linger requires a touch of magic, but it's absolutely within reach with a sprinkle of love and a dash of enthusiasm. Picture yourself in situations where you're living or working alongside individuals caught in the infectious web of negativity. Now, imagine setting vibrant boundaries that glow with positivity, serving as shields to protect your precious mental and emotional space. These boundaries gently guide conversations away from low energy emotions and towards the bright, sunny fields of positivity, where every word spoken can instead blossom into a celebration of life.

Picture yourself putting on the glasses of empathy, seeing through the eyes of those caught in negativity. The vision of empathy allows you to see their struggles, their fears, and their insecurities, and you respond not with frustration but with a warm embrace of compassion.

Most importantly, you can begin to realize that despite the storm raging outside, you hold the power to cultivate a garden of positivity within yourself. With each thought, each action, and each intention, you sow seeds of love, joy, and hope that blossom into a radiant bouquet of positivity. Your enthusiasm can become contagious. Your boundless love and your unwavering optimism can ignite a chain reaction of positivity that spreads like wildfire. Each act of kindness, each word of encouragement, and each smile you share can light up the darkness and transform it into a world of light.

Now, let's journey into the transcendent realm of meditation, a sacred practice that unlocks the depths of your consciousness and taps into your innate healing abilities. Add the power of thought and elevated emotions to the power of meditation, and you become unstoppable and limitless. The power of meditation has been recorded for centuries around the world. The healing power of meditation is profound and multifaceted, offering benefits for the mind, body, and spirit. Through the practice of meditation, individuals can access deep states of relaxation, inner peace, and profound healing.

I am fond of 6 well-known meditation styles that all hold a unique place in healing. Mindfulness Meditation, anchoring our attention to the 3D present moment. Loving-Kindness Meditation, or metta meditation, centers around the cultivation of love and compassion.

Through repeating phrases of kindness towards oneself and others, this practice nurtures a sense of empathy and goodwill and is a powerful tool for healing. Transcendental Meditation (TM) takes a different approach, guiding practitioners to delve into the depths of consciousness. This technique induces a state of deep relaxation and heightened awareness, facilitating profound mental and physical rejuvenation. From reducing anxiety, improving cognitive function, to powerful healing, TM opens doorways to inner realms of tranquility and insight. Breathwork Meditation harnesses the rhythmic flow of our breath to anchor our attention and calm the mind. By synchronizing our breath with specific patterns or techniques, we tap into our body's natural rhythms, fostering relaxation and clarity. Breathwork meditation offers a gateway to release tension, regulate emotions, and unlock our innate capacity for healing. Visualization Meditation creates mental images of our goals and dreams, we ignite the power of manifestation and intention. Whether envisioning success, abundance, health or inner peace, visualization meditation empowers us to shape our reality from the inside out. Walking Meditation encourages us to bring mindfulness into motion, savoring each step and sensation as we move through space. Walking meditation not only connects us with the rhythm of our bodies but also deepens our connection with the natural world, grounding us in the present moment.

I want to speak a little more on the transcendental type of meditation. It involves transcending the limitations of the three-dimensional senses and expanding awareness beyond the physical body. I was initially nervous about this type of meditation because I didn't want to lose control or let in dark entities when I left my body. After learning how to meditate in love, I now absolutely love this meditation because it is the closest I have been to the realm I was in since my near-death experience, without all of the tragedy surrounding it. Love energy is also powerful as a tool of protection. This type of meditation can give individuals access to the same place of endless possibilities that many near-death experiencers enter in an easy and non-traumatic way of energy in the limitless, creative space.

Transcendental meditation and certain forms of guided visualization, aim to take practitioners beyond the 3D senses and out of the body. These practices often involve deep relaxation and focused concentration, leading to altered states of consciousness where individuals may experience a sense of expansion beyond physical boundaries. These altered states of consciousness can be measured in the brain through electroencephalograms (EEGs).

Dr. Joe Dispenza, a leading authority on the science of meditation and healing, describes a state of meditation where practitioners enter into what he refers to as "nowhere." In this state, individuals transcend the limitations of time, space, and physical reality, experiencing a sense of pure consciousness and connection to the quantum field of potentiality. According to Dispenza, accessing this state of nowhere allows individuals to tap into their innate healing abilities and create profound shifts in their health and well-being. He also incorporates metta meditation to harness love's power to heal both ourselves and others.

Advanced meditators, through consistent practice and mastery of meditation techniques, can harness the power of their consciousness to influence their reality. This includes the ability to heal chronic illnesses and ailments by directing focused intention and energy towards the restoration of health and balance within the body. Practicing meditators may also experience heightened intuition, expanded awareness, and a greater sense of connection to the interconnectedness of all life.

People who heal in meditation practices know how to utilize the meditation to create profound healing experiences and how to bring that creation into the 3D human experience. When the brain and the heart are in coherence, the body is already working on healing corrupt pathways and signaling genes to be used in the manner they were built to. When the mind is in the quantum, in nowhere, in nothing, in the friendly darkness, anything can be created and found. The thought creates the possibility and then it can be found in the darkness. The possibility is a frequency and the frequency of it can be found in the darkness, or the creative void, as a reality. Once it is found, the practitioner can focus on the feeling of gratitude for it already happening. The feeling, and powerful emotion of gratitude then draws it to the individual's physical body. When the emotion has drawn it to the person, they then draw upon the knowledge of language to speak it into existence. Not just once, but throughout their thoughts, words and actions continually. The language that it has already happened so that the feeling and the emotion of those thoughts keep drawing that reality into existence. "What you are seeking, is seeking you."

Combining meditation with the use of positive, outcome-driven language can amplify the healing and manifestation process. By incorporating positive affirmations, visualizations, and intentions into meditation practices, individuals can reprogram their subconscious mind and align their thoughts and beliefs with their desired outcomes. This synergy between meditation and positive language accelerates the creation process, allowing individuals to manifest their intentions more rapidly and effectively. Meditation holds profound healing potential, allowing individuals to transcend physical limitations, access altered states of consciousness, and tap into their innate healing abilities.

Chapter 18

Sustained Creation

In the 22 years of seemingly constant shadow work, the strength training of the heart of gratitude, and the newly found language to meditate in a way that gets me into the void again, my healing story can, and will, be permanent this time. Your story can be too. The story doesn't end with one healing, our souls have come here for learning and evolving. Once you reach your miracle, don't stop searching for more. My constant search for more, the dates with the divine, don't just keep me healthy, but they keep me in awe, in wonder, and excited for even more of the unknown. I trust the divine unfolding of my experiences.

With my DBS system shut off and unneeded, I've been asked what I plan to do with it. I have stated I'd rather not go through another brain surgery to remove the leads, but perhaps one day I will have the battery removed from my chest. The reply was, "So, the leads will just go nowhere?" How funny I thought, only where there is nothing, in nowhere, does everything exist!

Through consistent practice and the integration of positive language, the possibly painful acts of shadow work, and the harnessing of the transformative power of meditation, you too can create profound shifts in your health, well-being, and reality.

Chapter 19

Step into Your Divine Journey of Healing

As we reach the culmination of our transformative journey, take a moment to reflect on the incredible path you've traversed to unlock your innate powers of healing. Throughout this journey, you've delved deep into the recesses of your soul, confronting the shadows that once held you captive. You've embraced the power of positive thought and language, harnessing the extraordinary potential of neuroplasticity to shape your reality. And you've tapped into the mystical and magical realm of meditation, unlocking the boundless healing energy that resides within you.

In every trial and tribulation, in every moment of doubt and uncertainty, remember that you are divinely guided. The universe has orchestrated every twist and turn of your journey, leading you toward the realization of your full potential. Every challenge you've faced, every obstacle you've overcome, has been a stepping stone on the path to your ultimate healing and transformation.

The keys to healing lie within the depths of your soul, waiting to be unlocked through the sacred practice of shadow work. By confronting your deepest fears, insecurities, and traumas, you've liberated yourself from the chains of the past, paving the way for profound healing and growth. Embrace the shadows as allies on your journey, guiding you toward wholeness and self-discovery.

But remember, healing is not just a journey of the mind and soul—it is also a journey of the heart. Cultivate a mindset rooted in optimism, self-belief, and unwavering faith, knowing that your thoughts and intentions have the power to shape your reality. Through the practice of positive thought and language, you'll manifest your deepest desires with clarity, conviction, and joy.

And finally, immerse yourself in the mystical and magical realm of meditation, where the infinite wisdom of the universe awaits. Through the sacred practice of meditation, you'll tap into the boundless healing energy that resides within you, transcending the limitations of the physical realm and accessing a state of pure awareness and connection to the divine. Embrace the transformative power of meditation as you embark on a journey of self-discovery and spiritual growth.

Behold Your Own Power

As you continue on your journey of healing and self-discovery, remember that you are never alone. The universe is conspiring in your favor, guiding you toward your highest potential with every step you take. Embrace the power within you, trust in the divine timing of your journey, and know that the keys to healing are always within your reach.

For those seeking more in-depth and personal guidance on their healing journey, I invite you to reach out to me at bri0nicllc.com. bri(zero)nicllc.com. As a certified practitioner in many of the modalities covered in this book and more, a Death Doula, and an experienced Spiritual Doula, I am here to support you through spiritual awakening, the breaking of soul contracts, the transition of end-of-life experiences, and most importantly, to teach you how to unlock your own divine powers of healing.

Embrace your divine journey of healing, dear reader, and step boldly into the radiant light of your true essence. May you find peace, joy, and fulfillment on your path, and may your journey be blessed with love, abundance, and endless miracles.